Hitler
Invades
Poland

1 September 1939

Hitler
Invades
Poland

1 September 1939

CHERRYTREE BOOKS

A Cherrytree Book

This edition published in 2008
by Cherrytree Book, part of
The Evans Publishing Group
2A Portman Mansions
Chiltern Street
London WIU 6NR

British Library Cataloguing in Publication Data
Malam, John.
   Hitler invades Poland. - (Dates with history)
   1.World War, 1939-1945 - Causes - Juvenile
   literature
   2.World War, 1939-1945 - Campaigns - Juvenile
   literature
   I.Title
   940'.5'3'11

ISBN 9781842345351

To contact the author, send an email to:
johnmalam@aol.com

Picture credits:

Corbis: 12, 19, 20, 21, 24, 25
Hulton Getty: 6, 7, 9, 10, 11, 14, 15, 26
Popperfoto: 8, 16, 17, 18
Topham Picturepoint: 13, 27, 29

Printed in China by WKT Co. Ltd

Contents

The day the world went to war

Wars change the course of history. They are fought by people who believe they are doing the right thing. Their dates are remembered and their leaders are praised as heroes, or hated as monsters.

During the 20th century, wars were fought like no others the world had seen before. They were world wars – armed conflicts that spread around the globe. Of these, the Second World War, fought over six years from 1939 to 1945, was the most costly war in history. More people died in this war than in any other. It is estimated that some 20 million soldiers, sailors, and aircrew lost their

A memorial at Dachau concentration camp, in remembrance of those who lost their lives between 1933-1945.

lives, and as many as 40 million innocent civilians died. The man responsible for this carnage was Adolf Hitler, and it began when his army of German soldiers invaded Poland on 1 September 1939.

From an unpromising start in life Hitler rose to become the leader of Germany – but he wanted more than that. His wish to make Germany a world power pushed the nations of Europe into a war, at the end of which he lay dead in the ruins of Berlin, his capital city. History is written by the winners of wars, not the losers, and it is history that has judged Adolf Hitler to be one of the world's most hated men.

People returning to their homes in the bombed-out city of Berlin, after the end of the Second World War.

Hitler's early years

Adolf Hitler as a baby in 1890.

Adolf Hitler was born on 20 April 1889, the fourth child of Alois Hitler and Klara Pölzl. He was born in the village of Braunau, in Austria, close to the border with Germany.

The Hitlers were a middle-class family, comfortably off, but not rich, and they could afford a cook and a maid. The family moved house several times during Hitler's early years, each time because his father's work as a customs officer took him to a new town.

Hitler's father was a respected member of the local community. He lived for his job and spent more time at work than with his family. When he was at home he was very strict. He had a bad temper and could be violent. He often hit his young son. Years later, Hitler said he had feared his father and had never loved him. On the other hand, he was totally devoted to his mother. She cared for him, looked after him, and took an interest in the things he liked. Despite this, Hitler's childhood was far from happy.

A view of Austria in the early 1900s – the country of Hitler's birth.

It wasn't only Hitler's home life that was troubled. His education was interrupted several times because of his family's frequent house moves. He went to five different schools and his work suffered because of this. His spelling, grammar and handwriting were all poor. Art seemed to be the only thing he was good at, and he dreamed of becoming a painter.

Hitler's teenage years were also difficult. When he was 14, his father died. And at 19, his beloved mother died.

Life and politics in Vienna

After his mother's death, Hitler moved to Vienna, the capital of Austria. He had visited the city before, when he had tried to get a place at art school, but was

not accepted. From 1908 to 1913 Hitler earned a meagre living in Vienna by making and selling drawings of buildings, and by doing odd jobs. He slept in shelters for the homeless, dressed in poor clothes and rarely shaved or had a bath.

Adolf Hitler during his Vienna years – he later described it as a time of 'misery and woe'.

It was during this time, when he was in his early 20s, that Hitler took an interest in politics. In Vienna's bars and meeting places people talked about society's problems, and what they believed caused them. Hitler listened. Everything that was wrong was blamed on a small group of people – the Jews. There was no truth in what people said, but this didn't stop them from voicing their anti-Jewish feelings. Hitler liked what he heard. He had conversations with people. When Hitler spoke, it was their turn to listen.

It was not new to hate the Jews. They had been persecuted in Europe since the Middle Ages, when false stories were told about them – from blaming them for the plague, to the murder of Christian children. In the late 1800s, German philosophers began to argue that the German people belonged to a master race, whose abilities would make their nation strong. These same thinkers said the Jews among them were weak, that they were 'scarcely human' and that they were 'vermin'. Newspapers began to call Jews the enemies of the German people.

From Vienna, Hitler went to live for a short while in the German city of Munich. Even though he was Austrian by birth, Germany became the country he loved the most.

The city of Munich, Germany, in the 1920s.

The First World War, 1914-18

On 28 June 1914, Archduke Franz Ferdinand, a member of the Austrian Royal Family who was next in line to the throne of Austria, was assassinated. His death marked the start of the First World War.

Even before the murder of Franz Ferdinand, there was tension between the countries of Central Europe. In February of that year, Hitler had been called up to serve in the Austrian army. When doctors examined him they decided he was not fit enough to become a soldier.

Archduke Franz Ferdinand of Austria and his wife, Sophie, seen in Sarajevo minutes before they were assassinated.

Fighting started in August 1914 and Hitler managed to join the German army, fighting against Britain and France. Despite what the Austrian doctors had said, he made a good soldier.

Germany lost the First World War. It was a turning point in Hitler's life. He looked forward to a day when Germany would be strong again. He knew that people took notice of him when he spoke at meetings:

During the First World War, Adolf Hitler (right) fought in 47 battles and was awarded medals for bravery.

perhaps he could put this talent to use for the good of Germany.

After the war, Hitler returned to Munich. The city had become a centre for political activity in Germany. Many groups of activists were based there, one of which was the **German Workers' Party**. Hitler was asked by the German army to spy on this group and find out what it was up to. He found he had a lot in common with the German Workers' Party. Like him, they hated the Jews, loved Germany, and dreamed of their defeated nation rising again.

The rise of the Nazi Party

In 1919, Hitler decided he would go into politics. He joined the German Workers' Party as member number 55. Hitler thought he could turn this small group of people into a political party – a force to be reckoned with.

When Hitler joined the party it was little more than a few people who talked about what they believed in, without actually changing the way society worked. It had no grand plan. Hitler changed all this.

He began to use his power of speech to influence the

An artist's impression of Hitler speaking at an early meeting of the German Workers' Party in the 1920s.

way people thought. At his first speech for the party, in October 1919, there were just 111 people in the audience. Then, on 24 February 1920, more than 2,000 people came to listen to him. At this meeting Hitler gave the party a new name – the National Socialist German Workers' Party. Hitler was its leader. It soon became known as the **Nazi** Party, from its German name: *Nationalsozialistische Deutsche Arbeiterpartei.*

Hitler's Nazi Party became popular with many Germans, and thousands joined it. Nazis believed that the German people were a 'chosen race', superior to all other people. They believed that Germany had been punished too much at the end of the First World War and that Jews should have nothing to do with the running of German society. They believed Germany should become a great nation once more and that Germany should be led by one powerful German, whom they would call 'the **Führer**' (the leader).

The swastika – the infamous symbol of the Nazi Party.

The Nazi Party adopted a crooked cross, known as a **swastika**, as its symbol. Members welcomed each other with the word *Heil!* (Hail!), and a straight-armed salute.

A failed revolution

The early 1920s were troubled years for Germany. The country's economy was in ruins, and the government, based in the German capital of Berlin, was unpopular. Nazis believed it was controlled by Jews and by people who had very different political beliefs to their own, especially the **Communists** whom they hated. Hitler saw this as his chance to lead the Nazi Party to power and to finally become the leader of Germany.

Hitler in prison at Langeberg.

On 8 November 1923, Hitler and his supporters attempted to start a revolution in Munich. They hoped it would spread throughout Germany and lead to the downfall of the government. The following day, Hitler led 2,000 Nazis through the streets of Munich in an attempt to take control of the city. The police opened fire, and sixteen Nazis were shot dead. Hitler suffered a dislocated shoulder. Two days later he was arrested and charged with treason. At his trial he was given a five-year prison sentence.

Hitler used his time in prison to write the first part of a book, which he called *Mein Kampf* (My Struggle). It was the story of his life, his beliefs and his thoughts about the future of the German people.

Hitler's book became a best seller. Anyone with any interest in Nazi ideas wanted to read it and learn from it. By 1939, *Mein Kampf* had been translated into eleven languages and more than five million copies had been sold.

A young woman tidying a display of Hitler's book, **Mein Kampf,** *in a bookshop, 1940.*

Hitler's rise to power

After just nine months in prison, Hitler was released. As well as writing his book he had used his time in prison to think about the mistakes he had made. He still wanted to be Germany's leader, but he decided he should not use force to get what he wanted. Instead, he decided that he needed to be voted into power by the people of Germany.

Adolf Hitler waves to the cheering crowds after his victory in the 1930 elections.

The failure of the revolution had damaged the Nazi Party. Supporters had lost interest and drifted away. Hitler worked hard at rebuilding the party and turned it into a powerful political force. In the German elections of 1930, six million people voted for the Nazi Party, and 107 Nazis were elected to the **Reichstag**, the German parliament, in Berlin. The Nazi Party had become the second largest political party in Germany.

In 1932 Hitler became a German citizen and in that year's elections the Nazi Party won more votes than any other party. Fourteen million Germans voted for them, and 230 seats were won in the Reichstag, making the Nazi Party Germany's largest political party. Then, on 30 January 1933, Hitler was appointed **Chancellor** – the leader of the German government. He had got what he wanted.

At the age of 43, Adolf Hitler had become the most powerful man in Germany. He had used his skills as a public speaker to win support for his policies, and the German people had voted him into power. They believed that he would make Germany great once more.

Hitler is sworn in as Chancellor of Germany in 1933.

The Third Reich

Germany had a long and impressive history. Twice in the past there had been German empires. When the Nazi Party came to power in 1933, Hitler said it was the beginning of the **Third Reich** (Empire). He told the German people it would be the greatest of all the empires and would last 1,000 years.

The Reichstag building, the heart of the German government in Berlin, on fire in 1933.

One night in February 1933, shortly after Hitler had become Chancellor, a fire destroyed the Reichstag building. The Nazis blamed the Communists for starting it, as they were hated almost as much as the Jews. Some people said the Nazis themselves had started it. Whoever did it, Hitler used it to his advantage. He spoke fiercely against people he said were opposed to the Nazi Party and the future of Germany. More Germans than ever before believed him, and in the March 1933 elections, 17 million people voted for the Nazi Party. It was enough to give Hitler total control of the government. He had become an elected **dictator**. Hitler banned all other political parties, and he took power away from the trade unions. People who dared to speak against him or the Nazi Party were beaten, imprisoned in concentration camps, or killed.

On 30 June 1934, almost 400 Nazis whom Hitler thought might take power from him were killed. That murderous night is known as the **Night of the Long Knives**.

As his control over people's lives grew stronger, the Nazi greeting changed from *Heil*! to *Heil Hitler*! Teachers started the day's school lessons by saying it to their classes, and children were expected to call it out up to 150 times a day. The swastika symbol was seen everywhere. Hitler was starting to make his dream come true.

*A group of children greet Hitler with the Nazi **Heil Hitler**! salute.*

The build-up to war

The build-up to the Second World War began in June 1919, the year after the end of the First World War. In that year, a defeated Germany had been made to sign the **Treaty of Versailles**. It stated exactly how Germany was to be punished.

Under the terms of the Treaty of Versailles, German land was given to other European countries – Poland, France, Belgium and Denmark. The army was reduced to 100,000 men, the navy was only allowed six warships, and there was no air force. French and British soldiers were stationed in a part of Germany known as the Rhineland, and German soldiers were not allowed there. Germany was told to pay for the damage caused by the war and to accept the blame for starting it.

The Treaty of Versailles humiliated Germany. The German people thought they had been punished far too severely.

Almost as soon as Hitler came to power in 1933, he made it clear that he was going to ignore the terms of the Treaty of Versailles. He began to re-arm Germany. He formed an air force and built up the strength of the army. In March 1936 he sent his soldiers into the Rhineland. He announced his intention to take back the German land that had been given to other countries.

A map of Central Europe after the First World War.

In March 1938, Austria joined with Germany. It was the first real move made by Hitler to form the Third Reich. He still had strong feelings towards the country of his birth and when the two countries came together, Hitler said it was the proudest hour of his life.

Hitler then turned his attention to the German-speaking area of **Sudetenland**, a region of Czechoslovakia. It had once belonged to Austria, but had been given away in 1919. At the end of September 1938, a treaty was signed and during the first week of October, German soldiers moved into Sudetenland. It was another victory for Hitler. His next target was Poland.

Hitler invades Poland

By the autumn of 1939, the German armed forces totalled more than 4.5 million men in the army, air force and navy. They were well-trained and had good

Polish cavalrymen on horses, carrying swords and lances, stood no chance against Germany's superior firepower and tanks.

equipment. The air force had more than 2,500 modern fighter and bomber planes. Germany had become the best-armed country in Europe.

The Second World War began at dawn on 1 September 1939, when around 1 million German troops crossed into Poland at three places, and some 1,500 warplanes went into action. Again, Hitler claimed it was to take back land that had once belonged to Germany. Poland's out-dated forces were no match against the German troops.

The German army advanced rapidly across Poland, heading for Warsaw, the country's capital. By 16 September, Warsaw was surrounded. For the next 11 days the city came under intense bombardment from the German air force and from artillery on the ground. On 27 September, Poland surrendered.

It had taken Germany just four weeks to defeat Poland, in what Hitler called a '**blitzkrieg**', meaning 'lightning war'. It was a totally new type of attack, which combined air and ground forces with speed, surprise, good communications and clever battle tactics. Hitler's lightning war against Poland was so successful that only 8,000 German troops were killed, compared with around 70,000 Poles.

The world had sat back and watched as Hitler had risen to power, then ignored the terms of the Treaty of Versailles and taken control of Austria and Sudetenland. However, the invasion of Poland was seen as an outrage – it was nothing less than an act of war and Hitler had to be stopped.

German soldiers march through the streets of Warsaw, Poland, in a victory parade.

Defeat for Germany

On 3 September, two days after Hitler's troops had invaded Poland, Britain and France declared war on Germany. Germany dominated the beginning of the war. Many countries – Denmark, Norway, the Netherlands, Belgium, Luxembourg, France, Yugoslavia, and Greece – fell to Germany, and the German air force raided towns and cities in Britain.

Then, in 1941, Germany invaded Russia, and also declared war on the USA. However, in 1943, the Germans in Russia surrendered. Soon after this, the Germans in North Africa surrendered. In 1944, an invasion force of British and American troops landed in northern France. While they started to push the German army back from the west, the Russian army pushed the Germans back from the east. By 1945, much of Europe had been freed from German control, and the armies of Britain, America and Russia closed in on Berlin, the German capital.

Soldiers read the news that Britain and France have declared war on Germany.

In the closing days of the war, Hitler took refuge in an underground **bunker** in Berlin. It was here, on 29 April 1945, that he married his long-time companion, Eva Braun. The next day Adolf Hitler and Eva Braun killed themselves. In accordance with Hitler's will, their bodies were burned and then buried. One week later, on 7 May 1945, Germany surrendered, and the war in Europe came to an end.

The true horror of the war then emerged as the Nazis' '**Final Solution**' was uncovered. Between 1941 and 1945, Jews from all over Europe were rounded up and sent to special camps, where they were gassed to death. More than 6 million Jews died in the concentration camps. Today, the very mention of 'Nazi' and 'Hitler' is enough to remind the world of the evils of war.

Jewish prisoners in a German concentration camp.

Timeline

1889   *20 April:* Adolf Hitler is born at Braunau, Austria.

1903   *3 January:* Hitler's father, Alois, dies.

1905   Hitler leaves school.

1907   Hitler is turned down for art school.

1908   *21 December:* Hitler's mother, Klara, dies. He moves to Vienna and tries to work as an artist.

1913   Hitler moves to Munich, in Germany.

1914   *February:* Refused entry to the Austrian army.

1914   *4 August:* First World War begins. Hitler joins the German army.

1914   *December:* Awarded the Iron Cross Second Class.

1918   *August:* Awarded the Iron Cross First Class.

1918   *November:* First World War ends.

1919   *12 September:* Hitler attends a meeting of the German Workers' Party.

1920   *24 February:* Hitler calls the German Workers' Party the Nazi Party.

1920   *31 March:* Hitler leaves the army.

1921   *29 July:* Hitler becomes leader of the Nazi Party.

1923   *8-9 November:* Hitler attempts a revolution.

1924   Hitler goes to prison, where he writes *Mein Kampf.*

1930–32 The Nazi Party becomes Germany's main political party.

1933 *30 January:* Hitler becomes Chancellor. The Third Reich begins.

1933 *27 February:* The Reichstag building is damaged by fire.

1934 *30 June:* Hitler kills his enemies in the Night of the Long Knives.

1936 *7 March:* Hitler's troops move into the Rhineland.

1938 *12 March:* Invasion of Austria.
October: Hitler's troops move into the Sudetenland.

1939 *1 September:* Invasion of Poland. The Second World War begins.

1945 *30 April:* Hitler shoots himself.

1945 *7 May:* Germany surrenders. War in Europe ends.

Soviet soldiers put up their flag over the Reichstag in Berlin after the Germans surrender.

Glossary

blitzkrieg A German word meaning 'lightning war', used to describe a rapid and successful advance into enemy territory.

bunker An underground shelter, made of steel and concrete.

Chancellor The head of state of Germany.

Communist A member of a political movement that believes a country's economy should be owned by the people as a whole, not by a few privileged individuals.

dictator A person who rules a country with absolute power, and who prevents any opposition.

'Final Solution' The Nazi term used for the murder of Jews.

Führer A German word meaning 'leader', adopted by Hitler as his official title in 1931.

German Workers' Party A political party which Hitler transformed into the National Socialist German Workers' Party (the Nazi Party).

Nazi A member of the National Socialist German Workers' Party (the Nazi Party).

Night of the Long Knives 30 June 1934, when Hitler ordered the murder of some 400 Nazis who opposed him.

Reichstag The German parliament, in Berlin.

Sudetenland A mountainous region taken from Austria at the end of the First World War and given to Czechoslovakia. It was given to Germany in 1938.

swastika A crooked black cross which became a symbol of the Nazi Party in 1919.

Third Reich The term adopted by Hitler to describe the 1,000 year empire he hoped to create for Germany.

Treaty of Versailles The peace treaty signed in 1919 at Versailles, near Paris, France, which redrew the map of Europe after the end of the First World War.

Index